Salter Dual Air Fryer Cookbook for Beginners

1000-Days Simple, Quick, and Delicious Dishes for Busy People on a Budget - Anyone Can Cook.

Akina Andra

Table of Contents

Chapter 7: Frittatas, Quiches and Casseroles 94

INTRODUCTION

We enjoy air fryers partly because of the creative features frequently provided to swiftly and evenly cook items. With dual-drawer air fryers, you can simultaneously prepare two different foods while the appliance manages the timing to guarantee that everything is done simultaneously. Or, for large households, make twice as much food with far less oil.

The Salter dual-drawer air fryer is a good option for anyone looking to upgrade their frying capacity from a single-drawer model at an affordable price because it is on the lower end of the price spectrum. It is also smaller than you may imagine, with dimensions of 40 cm, 36 cm, and 32 cm.

It fits beneath low-hanging kitchen cabinets for countertop storage and is only 10 cm longer than many of the single-drawer variants we are familiar with. This dual-drawer air fryer is an excellent value if you don't mind a little trial and error to get the perfect cook for your favorite foods.

This cookbook contains delicious, easy, and healthy recipes that are well prepared.

Grab this cookbook right now and start living a healthy lifestyle.

Chapter 1: Appetizers and Snacks

Delicious Pitta Pizza

Prep Time: 5 Minutes Cook Time: 8 Minutes Serves: 4

Ingredients:

- 4 tbsp gluten-free BBQ sauce
- 80g grated cheddar cheese
- 4 gluten-free pitta bread
- 60g diced cooked chicken
- 40g sliced mini pepperoni
- 40g diced red pepper
- 80g diced mozzarella
- Pinch chili flakes

Directions:

1. Spread the BBQ sauce over each pitta bread.
3. Sprinkle on the cheddar and mozzarella.
4. Top each pitta with the chicken, pepperoni, red pepper, and chili flakes.
5. Cook the pittas one at a time in your air fryer at 180°C (356°F) for 7 minutes.
6. Repeat until all the pizzas are cooked.
7. Serve with salad.

Nutritional Value (Amount per Serving):

Calories: 215; Fat: 12.67; Carb: 9.51; Protein: 15.63

Smoked Fish Pie with Gnocchi Topping

Prep Time: 10 Minutes Cook Time: 30 Minutes Serves: 4

Ingredients:

- 340g pack fish pie mix, salmon, smoked haddock, and white fish
- 100ml vegetable stock, made with one stock cube
- 1 tbsp corn flour, mixed with1 tbsp cold water
- 5g fresh flat-leaf parsley, chopped
- 500g shop-bought fresh gnocchi
- 180g tub of soft cheese
- 75g frozen sweetcorn
- 2 tbsp vegetable oil
- Salt and black pepper
- 75g frozen peas

Directions:

1. Place the cream cheese into a bowl, add the stock and corn flour mixture, and whisk well until combined. Season with salt and pepper then gently stir in the fish.
2. Transfer to a roasting tin that fits into the air fryer, approximately 22cm x 22cm x 5cm deep.
3. Place the dish onto the air fryer tray and set the fryer temperature to 180°C (356°F) for 10 minutes.
4. Place the gnocchi in a bowl and toss them with the oil so that the gnocchi are fully coated.
5. Remove the fish pie from the air fryer and stir through the peas, sweetcorn, and ¾ of the parsley.
6. Place the gnocchi evenly over the fish pie and return to the air fryer set to 190°C (374°F) for 15-20 minutes until the sauce is bubbling and the gnocchi is crisp and golden.
7. Sprinkle with the remaining parsley and serve with some fresh seasonal vegetables.

Nutritional Value (Amount per Serving):

Calories: 701; Fat: 47.43; Carb: 36.29; Protein: 34.58

Dino Nuggets in Air Fryer

Prep Time: 0 Minute Cook Time: 15 Minutes Serves: 4

Ingredients:

➢ 500g frozen dino nuggets
➢ Dipping sauce of choice

Directions:

1. Remove the frozen dinosaur nuggets from the packaging.
2. Arrange them in the air fryer basket, making sure you are not stacking them.
3. Cook the nuggets for 8-10 minutes until crispy and golden on the outside, flipping the basket or flipping the nuggets halfway through
4. Serve immediately with a side of fries, mashed potatoes, veggies, and a dipping sauce of choice

Nutritional Value (Amount per Serving):

Calories: 159; Fat: 4.5; Carb: 27; Protein: 3.75

Chicken Kebabs

Prep Time: 10 Minutes Cook Time: 20 Minutes Serves: 8

Ingredients:

- 150 ml BBQ sauce or other sauce of choice
- 2 white or red onions your choice
- 400g chicken breast or thigh
- 3 peppers bell peppers
- Salt and pepper

Directions:

1. Cut the chicken breast lengthways into 1-inch-thick strips.
2. Cut the onion into quarters. Remove the smallest centerpieces.
3. De-seed the peppers and cut them into large chunks, around 1 inch.
4. Place the chicken into a bowl, add the BBQ sauce (or other sauce), and then place it into the fridge for a minimum of 1 hour.
5. Layer up your skewers. I like to do pepper, chicken breast, onion, pepper, chicken breast, and onion, and repeat.
6. I place the chicken onto the skewer in an "S" formation, which I achieve by skewering the bottom of the chicken strip, then the middle folded over, then I fold again and skewering the top of the chicken breast.
7. I place the skewers into the air fryer basket and then cook at 200°C (390°F) for 20 minutes. At the 10-minute mark, I spray lightly with spray oil to keep them from becoming dry.

Tips:

You can use wooden skewers if you don't have a kebab rack, or don't want to buy one, but soak them first to avoid them burning in the air fryer.

Nutritional Value (Amount per Serving):

Calories: 439; Fat: 15.79; Carb: 63.36; Protein: 19.14

Spiced Lentil Shepherd's Pie

Prep Time: 15 Minutes Cook Time: 45 Minutes Serves: 4

Ingredients:

- 175g chestnut mushrooms, washed and roughly chopped
- 1 medium carrot, peeled and finely diced
- 400g can finely chopped tomatoes
- 1 stick celery, finely diced
- 1 medium onion, diced
- 2 tbsp vegetable oil
- ½ tsp chili powder
- 2 tsp ground cumin
- 2 tbsp tomato puree

Vegetable stock:

- 1 tbsp corn flour, mixed with 2 tbsp cold water
- 2 x 400g cans of lentils, drained and rinsed

Topping:

- 1.2kg sweet potato, peeled and diced into 2cm chunks
- 20g vegan spread

Directions:

1. Put the carrot, onion, and celery into a 23cm square roasting tin and drizzle over the oil.
2. Put onto the air fryer tray, set the air fryer temperature to 180°C (356°F), and cook for 8 minutes, until the vegetables have softened. Stir halfway through.
3. Stir in the mushrooms and spices to the roasting tin and mix well. Cook for a further 5 minutes.
4. Add tomato puree, canned tomatoes, stock, lentils, and corn flour.
5. Return to the air fryer and continue to cook for 18 minutes.
6. Meanwhile, boil the sweet potatoes for 15-18 minutes, then drain, add butter, and mash until smooth. Season to taste.
7. Spread the mashed sweet potato over the lentil mixture.
8. Cook for 15 minutes at 190°C (374°F), until the sauce is bubbling and the potatoes are golden.

Nutritional Value (Amount per Serving):

Calories: 936; Fat: 42.63; Carb: 83.02; Protein: 65.55

Frozen Chicken Nuggets

Prep Time: 3 Minutes Cook Time: 10 Minutes Serves: 5

Ingredients:

> ➤ 30 frozen chicken nuggets

Directions:

1. Preheat the air fryer to 200°C (390°F) for 4 minutes.
2. Place frozen chicken nuggets in the air fryer basket, spreading them out in a single layer. No need to spray with oil.
3. Air-fry the frozen chicken pieces at 200°C (390°F) for 8-10 minutes, shaking the basket or turning the pieces halfway through (optional), until golden brown and cooked through.
4. Remove from the air fryer and serve with your favorite dipping sauce.

Nutritional Value (Amount per Serving):

Calories: 1051; Fat: 72.14; Carb: 49; Protein: 51.59

Air Fryer Prawns

Prep Time: 5 Minutes Cook Time: 5 Minutes Serves: 4

Ingredients:

- 30g Panko Breadcrumbs
- 300g Prawns, shelled
- ½ tsp Smoked Paprika
- ¾ tsp Garlic Granules
- 35g Breadcrumbs
- 35g Plain Flour
- 2 Eggs, beaten
- Cooking spray
- ½ tsp Cayenne
- ½ tsp Salt

Directions:

1. Combine flour with ½ tsp Garlic, ¼ tsp Smoked Paprika, ¼ tsp Cayenne and ¼ tsp Salt in a bowl.
2. Combine both breadcrumbs with ¼ tsp Garlic, ¼ tsp Smoked Paprika, ¼ tsp Cayenne and ¼ tsp Salt in another bowl.
3. Preheat the air fryer to 200°C (390°F).
4. Toss Prawns in the flour mixture. Then dip individually in egg and then breadcrumbs.
5. Repeat with remaining Prawns.
6. Lightly spray with cooking spray. Add a single layer of Prawns to the air fryer basket. Cook for 3 minutes.
7. Flip the Prawns and spray with more oil.
8. Cook for a further 2–3 minutes or until just cooked.
9. Repeat with remaining Prawns.

Nutritional Value (Amount per Serving):

Calories: 499; Fat: 21.87; Carb: 63.35; Protein: 11.75

Reheat French Fries in Air Fryer

Prep Time: 0 Minute Cook Time: 5 Minutes Serves: 1

Ingredients:

- ➢ Dipping sauce of choice to serve
- ➢ Leftover French fries

Directions:

1. Preheat the air fryer to 180°C (356°F) for 3 minutes.
2. Add the leftover to the air fryer basket in a single layer (avoid overcrowding the air fryer for a great result).
3. Reheat the fries for 3-5 minutes shaking the air fryer basket halfway through the cooking for even cooking.
4. Serve your reheated fries with any dipping sauce and enjoy.

Nutritional Value (Amount per Serving):

Calories: 14; Fat: 0.43; Carb: 2.3; Protein: 0.29

Flavorful Dynamite Shrimp

Prep Time: 5 Minutes Cook Time: 15 Minutes Serves: 6

Ingredients:

The Shrimp (Prawn) Marinade:
- 450g Shrimp (Prawns), deveined and shelled
- ½ tsp Red Chili Powder
- ½ tsp Salt
- 1 tbsp Soy Sauce
- 1 Egg
- 1 tsp Paprika
- 50g Buttermilk or another Egg

The Sauce:
- 115g Mayonnaise
- 1 tbsp Sriracha Sauce
- 3½ tbsp Sweet Chili Sauce

The Corn flour Mix:
- 75g Corn flour
- 120g Plain Flour
- 1 tsp Garlic Granules

Other:
- 1 tbsp Oil for brushing Prawns

Directions:

1. Combine Prawns with all the ingredients listed under Shrimp (Prawns) in a bowl and set aside.
2. Combine all the ingredients for the sauce in a small bowl and whisk together.
3. Combine all the ingredients for the Corn flour mix in a bowl and whisk together.
4. Preheat the air fryer to 200°C (390°F). Brush the inside of the air fryer with Oil.
5. Coat the marinaded Prawns in the Corn flour mix in batches.
6. Add to the air fryer leaving space between shrimp.
7. Cover and cook for 5 minutes. Flip and brush over some oil.
8. Cover and cook for 2–4 minutes or until cooked.
9. Drizzle sauce over the shrimp and serve immediately.

Nutritional Value (Amount per Serving):

Calories: 339; Fat: 13.44; Carb: 31.01; Protein: 22.33

Air Fryer Potatoes

Prep Time: 5 Minutes Cook Time: 22 Minutes Serves: 4

Ingredients:

- ➤ 5 Large Potatoes, peeled and cut into 3cm cubes
- ➤ 2-3 tbsp Oil
- ➤ Salt

Directions:

1. Bring a pot of water to a boil and carefully add Potatoes and a good pinch of Salt.
2. Boil for 12 minutes.
3. Preheat the unit and select Air Fryer mode.
4. Set the temperature to 200°C (390°F) and the timer to 10 minutes.
5. Then drain the potatoes in a colander. Shake and then add to the unit once ready.
6. Drizzle over the oil. Air fry for 10–15 minutes.

Tips:

Check if they are cooked through before serving. Season with more salt if needed.

Nutritional Value (Amount per Serving):

Calories: 430; Fat: 8.92; Carb: 80.58; Protein: 9.32

Chapter 2: Breakfast

Sourdough Bruschetta

Prep Time: 5 Minutes Cook Time: 10 Minutes Serves: 4

Ingredients:

- ➤ 1 small bunch of basil, leaves roughly chopped
- ➤ Sea salt and freshly ground black pepper
- ➤ 1 small red onion, finely chopped
- ➤ 4 slices of sourdough bread
- ➤ 3 tbsps. extra virgin olive oil
- ➤ 5 large vine tomatoes
- ➤ 1 tbsp balsamic vinegar
- ➤ 1 cloves garlic, crushed
- ➤ Salt and black pepper

Directions:

1. Cut the tomatoes in half and, using a teaspoon, remove the seeds and discard them.
2. Finely chop the tomatoes and place them in a mixing bowl.
3. Add the garlic, ¾ of the basil, red onion, and 2 tbsps. olive oil and balsamic vinegar.
4. Season with salt and black pepper and mix to combine.
5. Set the air fryer temperature to 200°C (390°F) and place the bread onto the air fryer tray, making sure that they are evenly spaced.
6. Toast the bread for 10 minutes, depending on how brown you like your toast.
7. Drizzle the warm toast with the remaining oil, top with the tomato mixture, then garnish with remaining basil leaves

Nutritional Value (Amount per Serving):

Calories: 563; Fat: 12.86; Carb: 85.25; Protein: 28.07

Tilapia Recipe

Prep Time: 5 Minutes Cook Time: 8 Minutes Serves: 2

Ingredients:

- ➢ 2 fillets of Tilapia
- ➢ 1 tsp Paprika optional
- ➢ ¼ tsp Garlic powder
- ➢ ¼ tsp Onion granules
- ➢ ¼ tsp Black pepper
- ➢ 1 tbsp Olive oil
- ➢ ½ tsp Parsley
- ➢ Salt to taste

Directions:

1. In a bowl, mix the salt, garlic powder, black pepper, onion granules, parsley, and paprika together.
2. Brush the fish with olive oil and sprinkle the seasoning on it.
3. Put the fish fillets in the air fryer, brush the top with olive oil, and sprinkle the seasoning all over the top as well.
4. And brush with olive oil.
5. Set the air fryer to 180°C (356°F).
6. Air fry tilapia for 8-10 minutes or until cooked through and flaky.
7. Remove carefully from the air fryer using a spatula.

Tips:

No need to flip tilapia during cooking. The spatula will help lift the fish fillet off the air fryer basket without breaking up.

Nutritional Value (Amount per Serving):

Calories: 130; Fat: 2.17; Carb: 4.28; Protein: 23.9

Tuna Pasta Melt

Prep Time: 15 Minutes Cook Time: 25 Minutes Serves: 4

Ingredients:

- 300g wholewheat penne pasta, cooked as directed on the pack
- 2 x 145g cans of tuna chunks in spring water, drained
- 2 tbsp corn flour, mixed with 2 tbsp cold water
- 50g half-fat cheddar cheese, grated
- 400ml hot vegetable stock
- 200g can sweetcorn, drained
- 140g frozen peas, defrosted
- 150g half fat crème fraiche
- 180g light fat soft cheese
- 1 tbsp Dijon mustard
- Salt and black pepper
- 1 tbsp chopped parsley

Directions:

1. To prepare the sauce, put the crème fraiche, soft cheese, corn flour, and mustard in a bowl and whisk to combine.
2. Stir in the hot stock, and season with a pinch of salt and black pepper.
3. Put the cooked pasta, tuna, peas, sweetcorn, and grated cheese into a 24cm x 5cm deep square roasting dish.
4. Pour the sauce over the pasta and stir gently to coat everything in the sauce.
5. Place the roasting tin on the cooking tray of the air fryer and set the temperature to 180°C (356°F) for 25 minutes.
6. Stir the pasta to melt halfway through cooking.
7. Serve in warm bowls and sprinkle the parsley over the tuna pasta melt.

Nutritional Value (Amount per Serving):

Calories: 1142; Fat: 105.1; Carb: 36.55; Protein: 23.62

Air Fried Boiled Eggs

Prep Time: 5 Minutes Cook Time: 12 Minutes Serves: 6

Ingredients:

➢ 6 eggs

Directions:

1. Set the temperature to 150°C (302°F) and set the time to 12 minutes.
2. Press START/STOP to begin preheating.
3. When the unit beeps to signify it has preheated, place eggs onto the air fryer tray.
4. Press the START/STOP to begin cooking.
5. Serve hot with toast or cold with a salad.

Tips:

If you prefer soft-boiled eggs, remove them at 8 minutes, if you prefer hard-boiled cook them for 12 minutes.

Nutritional Value (Amount per Serving):

Calories: 130; Fat: 9.64; Carb: 1.02; Protein: 8.97

Smoked Salmon, Scrambled Egg, and Avocado Toast

Prep Time: 5 Minutes Cook Time: 10 Minutes Serves: 4

Ingredients:

- 120g smoked salmon, roughly chopped
- 50ml single cream or whole milk
- 1 tbsp chopped chives, optional
- 4 slices of bloomer-style bread
- Scrambled Eggs
- 6 eggs
- 2 ripe avocados
- 10g butter
- Salt and black pepper

Directions:

1. Halve the avocado and remove the stone, then use a tbsp to scoop out the flesh into a mixing bowl.
2. Season with salt and black pepper and smash the flesh with a fork.
3. Set the air fryer temperature to 200°C (390°F) and place the bread onto the air fryer tray, making sure that the slices are evenly spaced.
4. Toast the bread for 8-10 minutes, depending on how brown you like your toast.
5. Meanwhile, in a jug lightly whisk together the eggs and cream, then stir through the chives and season.
6. Melt the butter in a non-stick frying pan and pour in the eggs.
7. Let the mixture sit for about 30 seconds, then stir with a wooden spoon. Allow to sit again for a few seconds, then stir and fold again, until the eggs are set and scrambled.
8. Stir ¾ of the salmon through the scrambled eggs and season to taste.
9. To assemble, spread the avocado evenly over the toasted bread, top with scrambled eggs and garnish with the remaining salmon.

Nutritional Value (Amount per Serving):

Calories: 661; Fat: 45.21; Carb: 20.42; Protein: 44.15

Chinese Kebabs Rice

Prep Time: 10 Minutes Cook Time: 20 Minutes Serves: 4

Ingredients:

- 1 Slice of Whole meal Bread (made into breadcrumbs)
- ½ Small Onion (peeled and diced)
- 1 tbsp Chinese Five Spice
- 100g Egg Fried Rice
- 150g Minced Pork
- 1 tsp Garlic Puree
- 1 tsp Tomato Puree
- 1 tbsp Soy Sauce
- Salt and Pepper

Directions:

1. Boil your Chinese rice in a pan once it is cooked with the same Chinese seasoning as used in the kebab.
2. Add a hardboiled egg and mix it well.
3. To make the kebabs place the second half of the seasoning in a mixing bowl.
4. Add the onion and mince and mix well.
5. Add the breadcrumbs and form them into sausage shapes.
6. Cook in the Air Fryer for 20 minutes on a 180°C (356°F) heat.

Nutritional Value (Amount per Serving):

Calories: 175; Fat: 8.89; Carb: 8.92; Protein: 14.15

The Ultimate Fried English Breakfast

Prep Time: 2 Minutes Cook Time: 20 Minutes Serves: 4

Ingredients:

- 8 Rashers Unsmoked Back Bacon
- 1 Can of Baked Beans
- 8 Medium Sausages
- 8 Slices of Toast
- 4 Eggs

Directions:

1. In the Air Fryer place your sausages.
2. Bacon in it and cook for 10 minutes at 160°C (320°F).
3. In one ramekin place the baked beans and in another your egg (ready for it to be fried).
4. Cook for a further 10 minutes at 200°C (390°F) until everything is cooked.
5. Dish up and serve.

Nutritional Value (Amount per Serving):

Calories: 409; Fat: 29.51; Carb: 10.44; Protein: 29.11

Boiled Eggs with Parma Ham Soldiers

Prep Time: 5 Minutes Cook Time: 10 Minutes Serves: 4

Ingredients:

- 8 asparagus spears
- 4 slices Parma ham
- Seasoning Your favorite
- Vegetable oil spray
- 4 eggs

Directions:

1. Bring a saucepan of water to a boil.
2. Wash and trim the ends from the asparagus and cook in boiling water for 2-3 minutes.
3. Drain then rinse under cold running water to cool.
4. Cut each slice of Parma ham in half and wrap a slice around each piece of asparagus, season and spray lightly with oil then lay on the air fryer tray.
5. Set the air fryer temperature to 200°C (390°F) and cook the asparagus for 8 minutes until the ham is crisp.
6. Meanwhile, bring a small pan of water to a boil, gently submerge the eggs into the water, and set a timer for 4 minutes for dippy eggs.
7. Remove from the pan, place in an egg cup, and serve with the crispy asparagus and Parma ham soldiers.

Nutritional Value (Amount per Serving):

Calories: 165; Fat: 11.55; Carb: 1.65; Protein: 13.02

Traditional Welsh Rarebit

Prep Time: 10 Minutes Cook Time: 15 Minutes Serves: 2

Ingredients:

- ➤ 2 Large Eggs (separated)
- ➤ 3 Slices of Bread
- ➤ 120g Cheddar
- ➤ 1 tsp Mustard
- ➤ 1 tsp Paprika

Directions:

1. Very lightly heat up the bread in the Air Fryer so that it is almost like toast. The best way to do this is to give it 5 minutes at 180°C (356°F).
2. Whisk the egg whites in a bowl until they form soft peaks.
3. Mix the egg yolks, paprika, cheese, and mustard in a bowl.
4. Then fold in the egg whites.
5. Spoon it onto the partly toasted bread.
6. Cook in the Air Fryer for 10 minutes at 180°C (356°F).

Nutritional Value (Amount per Serving):

Calories: 383; Fat: 26.03; Carb: 17; Protein: 20.3

Two Ingredient Croutons

Prep Time: 3 Minutes Cook Time: 8 Minutes Serves: 9

Ingredients:

➢ 2 Slices of Whole meal Bread
➢ 1 tbsp Olive Oil

Directions:

1. Chop your slices of bread into medium chunks.
2. Place them in the Air Fryer.
3. Add the olive oil and cook for 8 minutes on 200°C (390°F) heat.
4. Serve over your soup or as a snack.

Nutritional Value (Amount per Serving):

Calories: 25; Fat: 1.65; Carb: 2.2; Protein: 0.39

Chapter 3: Poultry

Prawn Paste Chicken Wings

Prep Time: 10 Minutes Cook Time: 20 Minutes Serves: 3

Ingredients:

- ➢ 300g Mid-joint Chicken Wings or Drumettes
- ➢ ½ tsp Chinese Rice Wine / Sherry
- ➢ 1 tbsp Prawn/Shrimp Paste
- ➢ 1 tsp Sesame Oil
- ➢ 1 tsp Ginger Juice
- ➢ 2 tbsp Olive Oil
- ➢ ¾ tsp Sugar
- ➢ Corn Flour

Directions:

1. In a bowl, combine prawn paste, sesame oil, sugar, ginger juice, and rice wine together until a paste is formed.
2. Marinade chicken with the sauce for at least an hour or preferably overnight in the fridge.
3. Coat the marinated chicken with corn flour.
4. Stir to coat evenly, shaking off excess flour on the chicken.
5. Preheat the air fryer to 180°C (356°F).
6. Meanwhile, lightly brush chicken pieces with olive oil.
7. Place the chickens into the air fryer. Cook for 8 minutes.
8. Pull out the tray, use tongs to turn the chicken pieces over, and cook for another 7 minutes.
9. Drain cooked chicken on paper towels before serving.

Nutritional Value (Amount per Serving):

Calories: 323; Fat: 23.38; Carb: 7.68; Protein: 20.14

Lemon Honey Chicken Stuffed with Zucchini

Prep Time: 10 Minutes Cook Time: 30 Minutes Serves: 4

Ingredients:

- ➢ 1 whole chicken

The Filling:

- ➢ 1 green zucchini
- ➢ 1 yellow zucchini
- ➢ 1 sweet apple
- ➢ 2 tbsps. olive oil
- ➢ 2 red onions
- ➢ 2 apricots
- ➢ Fresh thyme

The Marinade:

- ➢ Juice of 1 large lemon
- ➢ Freshly ground pepper
- ➢ 200g honey
- ➢ Salt

Directions:

1. Chop all the ingredients for the filling into small cubes and mix with the oil in a bowl.
2. Season to taste with salt and pepper. Fill the chicken with the mixture.
3. Heat the Air fryer to 200°C (390°F).
4. Place the chicken in the Air fryer and sear the meat for 5 minutes.
5. Meanwhile, melt the honey in a pan with the juice of the lemon and season it to taste with salt and pepper.
6. Take the chicken out of the Air fryer and cover it in some marinade.
7. Set the temperature of the Air fryer to 150°C (302°F) and put the chicken back in. Open the Air fryer every 15 minutes to cover the chicken with marinade until it has all gone.
8. After 60 minutes, the chicken will be cooked.

Tips:

If you have the grill pan accessory you can use this to place the chicken on, so you have more space in your Air fryer.

There are two ways to check whether the chicken is cooked. Either with a meat thermometer (temperature must be 85°C

(185°F)) or by checking the color of the liquid. When cooked, the liquid will run clear and show no pink.

Nutritional Value (Amount per Serving):

Calories: 834; Fat: 22.6; Carb: 59.79; Protein: 99.76

Chicken Fried Rice

Prep Time: 5 Minutes Cook Time: 20 Minutes Serves: 6

Ingredients:

- ➢ 5 tbsp tamari soy sauce or regular if not gluten-free
- ➢ 200g frozen veggies (used sweet corn and peas)
- ➢ 2 green onions (spring onions), sliced
- ➢ 130g chicken leftover and cubed
- ➢ 1 tbsp chili sauce optional
- ➢ 1 tsp sesame oil
- ➢ 1 tsp vegetable oil
- ➢ 325g rice cold
- ➢ Salt to taste

Directions:

1. Preheat the air fryer to 180°C (356°F).
2. Mix all the ingredients together in a large bowl.
3. Then transfer to a non-stick pan that fits inside the air fryer basket.
4. Cook for 20 minutes, stirring the rice mixture a couple of times during cooking.
5. Enjoy it while it's hot

Nutritional Value (Amount per Serving):

Calories: 104; Fat: 3.41; Carb: 15.69; Protein: 2.97

Stuffed Chicken Breast Wrapped in Serrano Ham

Prep Time: 5 Minutes Cook Time: 30 Minutes Serves: 4

Ingredients:

- ➤ 100g soft cheese with garlic and herbs
- ➤ 4 medium chicken breasts
- ➤ 4 slices Serrano ham
- ➤ Vegetable oil spray
- ➤ Salt and black pepper

Directions:

1. Using a sharp knife, cut a pocket in the fattest part of each chicken breast then fill it with equal amounts of the cheese.
2. Season the chicken with salt and black pepper.
3. Wrap the chicken breasts with Serrano ham then place them on an airflow rack lined with parchment paper and spray lightly with oil.
4. Place the chicken on the air fryer tray and start the chicken program.
5. Check that the chicken breasts are cooked using a meat probe (the temperature should be over 75°C (167°F)) and extend the cooking time if necessary.
6. Remove the chicken from the air fryer onto a warm plate and cover it with foil for 5 minutes to rest.
7. Serving it with your favorite seasonal vegetables and roast potatoes.

Nutritional Value (Amount per Serving):

Calories: 558; Fat: 29.35; Carb: 3.66; Protein: 66.2

Spicy Drumsticks with Barbecue Marinade

Prep Time: 25 Minutes Cook Time: 20 Minutes Serves: 4

Ingredients:

- Freshly ground black pepper
- 1 clove garlic, crushed
- 2 tsps. brown sugar
- 1 tsp chili powder
- ½ tbsp mustard
- 1 tbsp olive oil
- 4 drumsticks

Directions:

1. Preheat the Air Fryer to 200°C (390°F).
2. Mix the garlic with the mustard, chili powder, brown sugar, a pinch of salt and freshly ground pepper to taste. Mix with the oil.
3. Rub the drumsticks completely with the marinade and leave to marinate for 20 minutes.
4. Put the drumsticks in the basket and slide the basket into the Air Fryer.
5. Set the timer to 10 minutes. Roast the drumsticks until brown.
6. Then lower the temperature to 150°C (302°F) and roast the drumsticks for another 10 minutes until done.
7. Serve the drumsticks with corn salad and French bread.

Nutritional Value (Amount per Serving):

Calories: 275; Fat: 19.81; Carb: 2.88; Protein: 20.54

Herby Chicken Thighs

Prep Time: 5 Minutes Cook Time: 30–40 Minutes Serves: 2-4

Ingredients:

- 4 chicken thighs, with skin on
- 2 level tsp dried oregano
- 2 level tsp dried thyme
- 2 tbsp lemon juice
- 5 tbsp olive oil
- 2 bay leaves
- Black pepper
- A little salt

Directions:

1. Prick the chicken all over with a fork and place in a shallow layer in a dish.
2. Sprinkle on the oregano and thyme, add the bay leaves and a generous grinding of black pepper.
3. Pour on the lemon juice and olive oil and turn the joints to coat them all over.
4. Cover the dish with foil, place in the fridge for at least 4 hours, turning from time to time.
5. Preheat at 180°C (356°F) for 3 minutes.
6. Discarding the marinade place the chicken into the frying basket.
7. Cook at 180°C (356°F) for 30 -40 minutes, turning halfway through cooking.
8. Ensure the chicken is fully cooked and that the juices run clear before serving.
9. Season the chicken with a little salt and serve on a bed of watercress with new potatoes or French fries.

Nutritional Value (Amount per Serving):

Calories: 775; Fat: 65.37; Carb: 2.65; Protein: 42.72

Roasted Chicken Wings

Prep Time: 5 Minutes Cook Time: 10 Minutes Serves: 4

Ingredients:

- ➢ 500g chicken wings at room temperature
- ➢ Freshly ground black pepper
- ➢ 100 ml sweet chili sauce
- ➢ 1 tsp ground cumin
- ➢ 2 tsps. ginger powder
- ➢ 2 cloves garlic

Directions:

1. Preheat the Air Fryer to 180°C (356°F).
2. Mix the garlic with the ginger powder, cumin, plenty of freshly ground black pepper and some salt.
3. Rub the chicken wings with the herbs.
4. Put the chicken wings in the basket and slide it into the Air Fryer.
5. Set the timer to 10 minutes and roast the chicken wings until they are crispy brown.
6. Serve the chicken wings with the chili sauce as a main course or a snack.

Nutritional Value (Amount per Serving):

Calories: 527; Fat: 32.3; Carb: 10.03; Protein: 45.52

Crispy Chicken Breast

Prep Time: 5 Minutes Cook Time: 10 Minutes Serves: 4

Ingredients:

- 450g skinless boneless chicken breasts halved crossways
- 50g gluten-free breadcrumbs or regular
- 4 tbsp grated parmesan cheese
- 1 tsp Italian seasoning
- ½ tsp ground coriander
- 1 tsp paprika
- Salt optional
- Cooking spray

Directions:

1. Preheat the air fryer to 180°C (356°F).
2. Mix together breadcrumbs, paprika, parmesan cheese, Italian Seasoning, ground coriander and salt in a bowl.
3. Lightly spray both sides of the halved chicken breast with a calorie-controlled cooking spray.
4. Cover both sides of the chicken breasts with the coating mix and place chicken breast in the air fryer basket. Make sure the chicken breasts are not touching.
5. Cook between 4-5 minutes then flip over and cook for 4-5 minutes on the next side.

Tips:

Cooking times depending on the thickness of the breast so maybe a little more or a little less. Chicken is done when it reaches an internal temperature of 75°C (167°F).

Nutritional Value (Amount per Serving):

Calories: 208; Fat: 4.71; Carb: 11.99; Protein: 27.87

Chicken Wrapped in Bacon

Prep Time: 3 Minutes Cook Time: 15 Minutes Serves: 6

Ingredients:

- ➢ 6 Rashers Unsmoked Back Bacon
- ➢ 1 tbsp Garlic Soft Cheese
- ➢ 1 Small Chicken Breast

Directions:

1. Chop up your chicken breast into six bite sized pieces.
2. Lay out your bacon rashers and spread them with a small layer of soft cheese.
3. Place your chicken on top of the cheese and roll them up.
4. Secure them with a cocktail stick.
5. Place them in the Air Fryer for 15 minutes on a 180°C (356°F) heat.

Nutritional Value (Amount per Serving):

Calories: 99; Fat: 5.98; Carb: 0.32; Protein: 10.64

Grilled Chicken Sticks

Prep Time: 10 Minutes Cook Time: 30 Minutes Serves: 4

Ingredients:

- ➢ 5 Green Onions (spring onions)
- ➢ 4 pieces Chicken Thigh Meat
- ➢ 8 Bamboo Skewer Sticks
- ➢ 60ml Soy Sauce (light)
- ➢ 1 tsp Sugar
- ➢ 1 tbsp Mirin
- ➢ 1 tsp Garlic Salt

Directions:

1. Soak bamboo sticks in water for 15 minutes.
2. Cut chicken into 1" square pieces.
3. Cut green onions into 1" length.
4. Stick chicken and onion in alternate orders into skewers
5. In a mixing bowl, add soy sauce, garlic salt, Mirin and sugar. Mix well.
6. Marinate chicken with sauce for at 2 hours,
7. Preheat air fryer for 5 minutes at 180°C (356°F).
8. Place skewers into air fryer and cook for 12 minutes.

Nutritional Value (Amount per Serving):

Calories: 413; Fat: 10.73; Carb: 36.52; Protein: 42.56

Chapter 4: Meats

Thai Meatballs

Prep Time: 5 Minutes Cook Time: 10 Minutes Serves: 2

Ingredients:

- 1 kg Minced Pork/Ground Pork
- 1 tbsp Philadelphia Light Herbs
- 1 tbsp Thai 7 Spice Seasoning
- Soup Maker Lentil Soup
- ½ Medium Red Onion
- 2 tsp Garlic Puree
- ½ tsp Ground Ginger
- 5 Kaffir Lime Leaves
- Salt and Pepper

Directions:

1. Thinly slice your Thai leaves. Peel and thinly dice your red onion.
2. Load into a bowl all your meatball ingredients and mix with your hands for a well coating of the seasoning and the onion.
3. Make into Thai balls using the measuring scales to get equal sized meatballs. 47g each.
4. Do all meatballs and then cook them in batches to what will fit in your air fryer.
5. Load the Thai meatballs into the air fryer basket and air fry for 10 minutes at 180°C (356°F).
6. When the air fryer beeps serve your Thai meatballs over your lentil soup before serving.

Nutritional Value (Amount per Serving):

Calories: 1016; Fat: 68.58; Carb: 34.12; Protein: 67.87

Air Fryer Brisket

Prep Time: 5 Minutes Cook Time: 45 Minutes Serves: 4

Ingredients:

- 1 tbsp Extra Virgin Olive Oil
- 1.2 kg Beef Brisket
- 2 tsp Rosemary
- 2 tsp Basil
- 2 tsp Parsley
- 2 tsp Thyme
- Salt and Pepper

Directions:

1. Place the beef brisket in a tray for easy seasoning.
2. Then smoother with extra virgin olive oil and then smoother with the seasonings. The dried seasonings will then stick to the oil and stay on the beef as it cooks.
3. If some comes off, then use the tray to roll the beef and grab any stray bits of seasoning.
4. Load into the air fryer basket and cook for 30 minutes at 180°C (356°F).
5. Turn over and cook for a final 15 minutes at the same temperature.
6. Then transfer to a chopping board for resting and remove the string.
7. Once the brisket has rested for 5-10 minutes slice before serving.

Nutritional Value (Amount per Serving):

Calories: 613; Fat: 46.27; Carb: 1.75; Protein: 44.28

Homemade Fishcakes

Prep Time: 10 Minutes Cook Time: 35 Minutes Serves: 4

Ingredients:

Cook The Fish:
- 1 Pink Salmon Fillet
- 1 Pollock Fillet
- 1 Cod Fillet
- 2 tsp Dill
- Salt and Pepper

Cook The Potatoes:
- 2 tsp Extra Virgin Olive Oil
- 300g Baby Potatoes
- Salt and Pepper
- 2 tsp Butter

Cake The Production Line:
- 480 ml Plain Flour/All Purpose
- 480 ml Breadcrumbs
- 2 tbsp Lemon Juice
- 2 Eggs beaten
- 1 tbsp Parsley
- 2 tsp Dill Tops
- 2 tsp Parsley
- 2 tsp Basil
- Salt and Pepper

The Fishcakes:
- 1 tbsp Fresh Parsley shredded
- 2 tsp Sweet Paprika
- 2 tsp Coriander
- 2 tsp Thai 7 Spice
- Salt and Pepper
- 1 tbsp Butter

Directions:

1. Place your mixed fish fillets in a bowl and let them sit for an

hour to get rid of any excess liquid. If they are frozen, you can defrost them in the bowl first.

2. Then remove the fish (minus the excess water) and place on a chopping board. Season well with salt, pepper, and dill.
3. Load the fish into the air fryer and cook for 8 minutes at 180°C (356°F)then place in bowl and use a fork to flake the fish.
4. In another bowl add baby potatoes, extra virgin olive oil and salt and pepper. Mix with your hands for an even coat.
5. Air fry for 17 minutes at 180°C (356°F) and then mash with a little butter. Add the mash to the cooked fish, and then add the fishcake seasoning list.
6. Use a fork or a masher to mash well and then once cool enough to touch make into Thai fish patties.
7. Though whilst you are waiting for them to cool set up your production line. Beaten egg in one bowl with lemon juice, flour and the 1tbsp of parsley in another bowl and the breadcrumbs and the rest of the seasoning in a third. Make sure all bowls are well mixed and that they are in the order of flour, egg, breadcrumbs.
8. Once you have made your Thai fish cakes load into the flour, into the egg and the breadcrumbs getting a good coating from each.
9. Load into the air fryer basket and air fry for 10 minutes at 180°C (356°F) or until fully heated through and you have a crispy breadcrumb texture.

Nutritional Value (Amount per Serving):

Calories: 1142; Fat: 22.67; Carb: 172.17; Protein: 58.9

Party Meatballs

Prep Time: 20 Minutes Cook Time: 15 Minutes Serves: 24

Ingredients:

- 2½ tbsp Worcester Sauce
- 3 Gingersnaps, crushed
- 50g Tomato Ketchup
- 1 tbsp Lemon Juice
- 50g Brown Sugar
- ½ tsp Dry Mustard
- 500g Mince Beef
- 1 tbsp Tabasco
- 60g Vinegar

Directions:

1. In a large mixing bowl place on your seasonings and mix well so that everything is evenly coated.
2. Add the mince to the bowl and mix well.
3. Form into medium sized meatballs and place them into your Air Fryer.
4. Cook them for 15 minutes on a 190°C (374°F)heat or until nice and crispy and cooked in the middle.
5. Place them on sticks before serving.

Nutritional Value (Amount per Serving):

Calories: 56; Fat: 1.61; Carb: 5.79; Protein: 4.66

Frozen Bacon in Air Fryer

Prep Time: 5 Minutes Cook Time: 20 Minutes Serves: 4

Ingredients:

- ➢ 620g Frozen Back Bacon

Directions:

1. Remove frozen bacon from the packaging and load into the air fryer basket.
2. Air fry for 8 minutes at 100°C (212°F). Turn every 2 minutes and strip the top and bottom slice and move each separated slice to a plate. Until you have all bacon rashers separated.
3. Load the defrosted bacon back into the air fryer basket and spread it out.
4. Air fry for 6 minutes at 200°C (390°F) turn with tongs and then air fry for the same time and temp on the other side.
5. Air fry for a little longer at 200°C (390°F) if it is not crispy enough as it will vary depending on the thickness of your bacon and how much you are air frying.

Nutritional Value (Amount per Serving):

Calories: 481; Fat: 45.76; Carb: 9.8; Protein: 16.55

Buffalo Tenders

Prep Time: 5 Minutes Cook Time: 10 Minutes Serves: 4

Ingredients:

- 350g Chicken Tenders
- 4 tbsp Plain Flour
- 2 eggs

Breadcrumb Coating:

- 75g Breadcrumbs
- 1 tsp Garlic granules
- ½ tsp dry Oregano
- 1 tsp Chili Flakes
- 1 tsp Smoked Paprika
- 1 tsp Black Pepper
- 1 tsp Salt

Buffalo Sauce:

- 120ml Hot Sauce (Franks Red Hot or Buffalo)
- 1 tsp Worcester Sauce (Optional)
- 2 cloves of Garlic, finely sliced
- 100g Butter
- Salt

Directions:

1. Add Eggs to a bowl and beat. Add Flour to another bowl.
2. Add Breadcrumbs and all the ingredients for breadcrumb coating to a third bowl and whisk together.
3. Add Chicken tender to the Plain Flour mixture, then to Egg mixture and then to the Breadcrumb mixture.
4. Preheat the Air Fryer to 200°C (390°F).
5. Once preheated, add the Chicken leaving a gap between each one. Spray with oil.
6. Cook for 10-12 minutes, turning midway and spraying again in between.
7. Melt the Butter for the Buffalo Sauce in a pan on the stove. Add the Garlic Cloves and Worcester Sauce.
8. Then whisk in the Hot Sauce. Taste and add Salt.
9. Empty Sauce into a bowl. Add the tenders and toss together to coat.

Nutritional Value (Amount per Serving):

Calories: 379; Fat: 21.89; Carb: 18.09; Protein: 26.07

Air Fryer Ham

Prep Time: 10 Minutes Cook Time: 45 Minutes Serves: 6

Ingredients:

- ➢ 1 tbsp orange juice or pineapple juice
- ➢ 1 kg boneless cooked ham
- ➢ 4 tsps. ground cinnamon
- ➢ 1 tsp dry mustard
- ➢ 3 tbsps. honey

Directions:

1. Preheat air fryer to 170°C (338°F).
2. Wrap ham in aluminum foil, making sure the overlapping foil sheets are on the top so you can open during cooking.
3. Transfer ham to the air fryer basket and air fry for 20 minutes.
4. In the meantime, in a small bowl mix together honey, orange juice, cinnamon and mustard powder.
5. When the 20 minutes is up, open up the ham and brush the sweet glaze all over the ham.
6. Then close up the foil and air fry for another 15 minutes. until the internal temperature reaches 60°C (140°F).
7. Open the foil and air fryer ham for a further 5 – 8 minutes or until glaze is nicely golden brown.
8. Remove from air fryer and let the ham rest for 15 minutes before carving.

Nutritional Value (Amount per Serving):

Calories: 320; Fat: 11.28; Carb: 11.89; Protein: 43.73

Tuna Steak

Prep Time: 5 Minutes Cook Time: 7 Minutes Serves: 2

Ingredients:

- 1 tbsp Extra Virgin Olive Oil
- 125g Cherry Tomatoes
- 1 tsp Oregano
- 2 Tuna Steaks
- 2 tsp Basil
- 1 tsp Thyme
- Salt and Pepper

Directions:

1. Half the cherry tomatoes and drizzle with extra virgin olive oil and season with salt, pepper, and basil.
2. Season tuna steaks with salt, pepper, oregano, and thyme and load into the air fryer basket.
3. Place cherry tomatoes in the gaps.
4. Cook for 7 minutes at 190°C (374°F).
5. After 7 minutes check to see if the tuna steak is cooked. If not cook for a further 2 minutes on the same temperature. Then follow this process if your tuna steaks are really thick.
6. Then serve the tuna steaks with the cherry tomatoes for a quick light lunch.

Nutritional Value (Amount per Serving):

Calories: 225; Fat: 4.96; Carb: 13.31; Protein: 33.93

Thick T Bone Steak

Prep Time: 2 Minutes Cook Time: 18 Minutes Serves: 2

Ingredients:

- ➢ 820g Thick T Bone Steak
- ➢ 2 tsp Sweet Paprika
- ➢ 2 tsp Parsley
- ➢ Salt and Pepper

Directions:

1. Place your t bone steak on a clean chopping board and allow it to go up to room temperature.
2. Season the t bone steak with salt, pepper, and half the sweet paprika and parsley.
3. Load into the air fryer.
4. Cook your t bone steak for 9 minutes at 180°C (356°F).
5. Turn the t bone over, season again and air fry for a further 9 minutes at the same temperature.
6. Then slice it open and it will be cooked to rare to medium.

Nutritional Value (Amount per Serving):

Calories: 951; Fat: 65.28; Carb: 3.55; Protein: 82.7

Pigs in Blanket

Prep Time: 1 Minute Cook Time: 8 Minutes Serves: 4

Ingredients:

- ➤ 4 rasher Streaky bacon
- ➤ 8 Chipolatas

Directions:

1. Slice the bacon in half.
2. Place the sausages at one end of each of the bacon rashers.
3. Roll the bacon around the sausages.
4. Spray the air fryer basket with some oil and place the pigs in blankets into it.
5. Cook at 180°C (356°F) for 8 minutes.

Nutritional Value (Amount per Serving):

Calories: 233; Fat: 2.36; Carb: 51.09; Protein: 2.17

Scallops With Cheese

Prep Time: 15 Minutes Cook Time: 10 Minutes Serves: 2

Ingredients:

- 60g Shredded Mozzarella Cheese
- 30g Butter (cubed, unsalted)
- 5 Half-shelled Scallops
- 2 tbsp Mayonnaise
- Black Pepper
- Salt

Directions:

1. Preheat air fryer at 200°C (390°F).
2. Remove scallop meat from the shell, rinse the meat thoroughly and remove any dirty bits.
3. Scald the scallop shells in hot water for a few minutes to disinfect, discard hot water and rinse the shells. Return scallop meat to the shell.
4. Place cubed butter in a small bowl and microwave for 40 seconds. Use a spoon to stir the butter vigorously to form a smooth paste. Add mayonnaise, salt and pepper, stir to combine well.
5. Place scallops on foil and place them into the air fryer. Cook for 5 minutes.
6. Using kitchen tongs, carefully drain the scallop broth collected in the shells in a small bowl.
7. Divide and spoon the mayonnaise mixture evenly among the scallops. Top with shredded cheese.
8. Return scallops to the air fryer and cook for another 8 minutes, or until the cheese is melted and slightly browned at the edges.

Nutritional Value (Amount per Serving):

Calories: 188; Fat: 13.54; Carb: 4.8; Protein: 11.85

Ground Beef

Prep Time: 2 Minutes Cook Time: 9 Minutes Serves: 2

Ingredients:

- 500g Ground Beef/Minced Beef
- 1 tsp Frozen Chopped Garlic
- 1 tsp Parsley
- Salt and Pepper

Directions:

1. Load into the air fryer basket your block of ground beef.
2. Sprinkle on the top the chopped garlic, pepper, salt, and parsley.
3. Air fry for 9 minutes at 180°C (356°F).
4. Though on the 3rd and the 6th minute break up the ground beef so that it has an even cook as it is air frying.
5. When the air fryer beeps drain the liquid from the bottom.
6. You now have perfectly cooked ground beef ready for adding to meals.

Nutritional Value (Amount per Serving):

Calories: 547; Fat: 27.84; Carb: 2.73; Protein: 66.99

Roast Pork

Prep Time: 10 Minutes Cook Time: 50 Minutes Serves: 3

Ingredients:

- ⅓ tbsp Shaoxing Wine (or Dry Sherry)
- ½ tsp Five-spice Powder
- 2 tsp Salt
- 600g Pork Belly
- 1½ tsp Sugar

Directions:

1. Use a knife to scrape away any impurities and hair from the pork belly. Rinse thoroughly.
2. Prepare the seasonings by combining salt with sugar and five-spice powder well.
3. Blanch pork belly in boiling water for about 12 minutes, or until 60% done, and the skin is softened.
4. Drain well and wipe dry. Cut a few slits on the meat to help absorb seasonings better.
5. Rub wine and seasoning evenly on pork. Make sure there's no seasonings on the rind, otherwise the five-spice powder will darken it.
6. Turn over, and wipe dry the rind. Use a fork to poke the rind as many holes as possible. Wrap the pork meat with foil and leave the rind unwrapped. Place in fridge, let air dry overnight in fridge.
7. Remove pork from fridge and let it rest in room temperature. Poke the rind with fork evenly once again. Wipe dry.
8. Preheat the air fryer for 5 minutes at 160°C (320°F). Place the pork belly skin facing up into the air-fryer. Cook for 160°C (320°F) for 15 minutes.
9. Take out and wipe dry the rind again. Continue at 180°C (356°F) for 30 minutes. Chopped into small bite-sized pieces.

Nutritional Value (Amount per Serving):

Calories: 1046; Fat: 106.02; Carb: 2.59; Protein: 18.73

Garlic Prime Rib

Prep Time: 5 Minutes Cook Time: 1 Hr. Serves: 6

Ingredients:

- 2 kg Prime Rib, remove the bones
- 1 tbsp Extra Virgin Olive Oil
- 1 tsp Garlic Powder
- Salt and Pepper

Directions:

1. Place your prime rib on a clean chopping board and cut to size to fit your air fryer.
2. Then smoother with extra virgin olive oil and then smoother with the seasonings. The dried seasonings will then stick to the oil and stay on the beef as it cooks.
3. Wrap in foil and place in the fridge overnight to marinade.
4. The next day remove the foil and load into the air fryer basket. If it's touching the top too much push down with your fingers to stop the top of the rib roast from burning.
5. Cook for 30 minutes at 180°C (356°F) and don't preheat the air fryer.
6. Turn over and cook for 20 minutes at the same temperature. It will now be a medium rare. Remove now if you would like medium rare.
7. For medium to well done turn the rib roast back over and cook for an extra 10 minutes at the same temperature.
8. Then transfer to a chopping board for resting before slicing and serving.

Tips:

Note your chopping board will be full of juices so you will want some kitchen towel ready.

Nutritional Value (Amount per Serving):

Calories: 1131; Fat: 98.29; Carb: 1.12; Protein: 56.01

Spicy Country Fries

Prep Time: 10 Minutes Cook Time: 20 Minutes Serves: 4

Ingredients:

- ½ tbsp freshly ground black pepper
- 800g waxy potatoes
- 2 small, dried chilies
- 1 tbsp olive oil

Directions:

1. Preheat the Air Fryer to 180°C (356°F).
2. Scrub the potatoes clean under running water. Cut them lengthwise into 1½ cm strips.
3. Soak the fries in water for at least 30 minutes.
4. Drain them thoroughly and then pat them dry with kitchen paper.
5. Crush the chilies very finely (in a mortar) and mix them in a bowl with the olive oil, pepper and curry powder. Coat the fries with this mixture.
6. Transfer the fries to the fryer basket and slide the basket into the Air Fryer.
7. Set the timer to 20 minutes and fry the fries until they are golden brown and done. Turn them every now and again.
8. Serve the fries in a platter and sprinkle with salt. Delicious with steak.

Nutritional Value (Amount per Serving):

Calories: 765; Fat: 44.19; Carb: 34.94; Protein: 54.3

Frozen Scallops

Prep Time: 5 Minutes Cook Time: 12 Minutes Serves: 2

Ingredients:

- 500g Frozen Raw Scallops
- 1 tbsp Fresh Parsley
- 6 Garlic Cloves
- Salt and Pepper
- 2 Lemons

Directions:

1. Remove the frozen scallops from the packaging, discarding any excess liquid and then place into the air fryer basket.
2. Season with salt and pepper.
3. Load up the air fryer with peeled garlic cloves, chopped parsley and lemon wedges.
4. Air fry for 12 minutes at 180°C (356°F).
5. Then check a scallop to make sure it is firm and has started to go light brown.
6. Then load onto a plate and squeeze the lemon juice from the lemons over the scallops and serve.

Nutritional Value (Amount per Serving):

Calories: 352; Fat: 9.25; Carb: 62.46; Protein: 8.63

Frozen Meatballs in Air Fryer

Prep Time: 1 Minute Cook Time: 15 Minutes Serves: 4

Ingredients:

- 1 package frozen meatballs any type
- Cooking oil or oil spray

Directions:

1. Remove your frozen meatballs from their outer packaging.
2. Place the frozen meatballs in the air fryer basket in an even layer.
3. Spray the meatballs with cooking oil.
4. Air Fry at 180°C (356°F) for 12-15 minutes, until the meatballs are heated through.
5. Serve immediately.

Nutritional Value (Amount per Serving):

Calories: 207; Fat: 1.73; Carb: 48.08; Protein: 12.11

Roast Beef

Prep Time: 5 Minutes Cook Time: 45 Minutes Serves: 4

Ingredients:

The Roast Beef:

- 1.2 kg roasting beef joint check it fits into your Air fryer
- 3 tbsp olive oil

Seasoning:

- ½ tsp mustard powder or brown sugar
- 1 tsp freshly ground black pepper
- ½ tsp dried thyme
- ½ tsp garlic granules
- ½ tsp dried rosemary
- 2 tsp coarse salt

Directions:

1. Take your beef joint out of the fridge and pat dry. Leave it to come to room temperature for 30 minutes.
2. Meanwhile, preheat the air fryer 200°C (390°F) for 10 minutes. Mix all the seasoning ingredients together and brush the beef all over with olive oil. Press the seasoning mix all over the beef.
3. Use a liner in the air fryer basket (optional) and position the beef on top. Roast for 10-15 minutes.
4. Remove the air fryer basket and turn the beef over. Reduce the temperature to 180°C (356°F) and cook for a further 30 minutes.
5. Start checking the internal temperature of the beef with an instant read thermometer inserting the probe in the middle thickest part. Use the table in the recipe notes as a guide to cook it to your liking, adding five minutes of cooking time until your preferred temperature is reached. Remember that the temperature of the joint will continue to rise slightly as it rests so factor that in. I usually aim for medium rare (55-57°C (131-135°F)).
6. Once the beef is cooked to your liking place it on a warm platter and cover loosely with foil.
7. Leave it to rest for 20-30 minutes before slicing against the grain and serving with your favorite side dishes.

Tips:

Cooking the beef at a high temperature will create a lovely crust on the exterior, sealing all the lovely juices within in the same way that searing the beef in a skillet before roasting in the oven.

Nutritional Value (Amount per Serving):

Calories: 679; Fat: 37.6; Carb: 3.49; Protein: 76.75

Pork Roast

Prep Time: 10 Minutes Cook Time: 1 Hr. 20 Minutes Serves: 4

Ingredients:

- ➤ 1 kg Air Fryer Sweet Potato Cubes
- ➤ 1.2 kg Pork Shoulder
- ➤ 1 tsp Garlic Powder
- ➤ 1 tbsp Olive Oil
- ➤ 1 tbsp Parsley
- ➤ Salt and Pepper

Directions:

1. Score your pork roast with similar sized square slits. Spray with extra virgin olive oil.
2. Season your pork with salt and pepper and your other seasonings.
3. Place the rod through the pork shoulder so that it has come through both ends. Secure the clamps on each side.
4. Place in the air fryer tray and make sure its secure.
5. Set the time to 1 hour and the temperature to 180°C (356°F).
6. When the air fryer beeps, remove from the air fryer to rest.
7. After it has rested for about 5 minutes remove the clamps and rod and allow to rest for 5 minutes before slicing.

Nutritional Value (Amount per Serving):

Calories: 943; Fat: 57.77; Carb: 23.79; Protein: 81.76

Chapter 5: Vegetables

Butter Carrots

Prep Time: 5 Minutes Cook Time: 15 Minutes Serves: 4

Ingredients:

- ➤ A pinch of salt and black pepper
- ➤ 450g carrots, cut into wedges
- ➤ ½ tbsp butter, melted
- ➤ 1 tsp sweet paprika

Directions:

1. In a bowl, combine all of the ingredients and toss well.
2. Put the carrots in your air fryer and cook at 176°C (348°F) for 15 minutes.
3. Divide between plates and serve.

Nutritional Value (Amount per Serving):

Calories: 90; Fat: 2; Carbs: 4; Protein: 4

Roasted Garlic

Prep Time: 5 Minutes Cook Time: 30 Minutes Serves: 2

Ingredients:

- ➢ 2 Tablespoons Extra virgin olive oil
- ➢ Salt to taste this is optional
- ➢ 2 garlic bulbs

Directions:

1. Preheat your air fryer to 190°C (374°F).
2. Cut some aluminum foil sheets that will be enough for the number of garlic heads you will be air frying.
3. Peel the papery outer layer of a garlic head, using a sharp knife cut about ½ inches of the garlic head so that top of all the cloves is exposed.
4. Place each garlic bulb on the prepared foil sheets
5. Drizzle a little bit of olive oil over the garlic, and then sprinkle with salt if using.
6. Wrap the foil around the garlic tightly to form a parcel.
7. Place the wrapped garlic in the air fryer tray, and cook for 20-30 minutes or until the cloves are soft and lightly golden brown.
8. Let the roasted garlic cool slightly before squeezing out the cloves to use in your dishes.

Nutritional Value (Amount per Serving):

Calories: 133; Fat: 13.64; Carb: 2.81; Protein: 0.54

Crispy Roast Potatoes

Prep Time: 5 Minutes Cook Time: 30 Minutes Serves: 4

Ingredients:

- ➤ 1kg potatoes, peeled and chopped into 4cm chunks
- ➤ Salt and ground black pepper
- ➤ 2 tbsp vegetable oil
- ➤ 1 tbsp plain flour

Directions:

1. Bring a large saucepan of water to the boil with a pinch of salt.
2. Add the potatoes to the boiling water and cook for 8-10 minutes until the edges have softened when you poke them with a knife.
3. Drain the potatoes in a colander and return them to the pan, sprinkle on the flour and oil then give the pan a shake to fluff up the potatoes.
4. Carefully transfer the potatoes into the air fryer basket.
5. Set the temperature to 180°C (356°F) for 20 minutes shaking them halfway through until the potatoes are crisp and golden.

Nutritional Value (Amount per Serving):

Calories: 593; Fat: 24.46; Carb: 46.27; Protein: 45.7

Hot Greek Potatoes

Prep Time: 5 Minutes Cook Time: 15 Minutes Serves: 4

Ingredients:

- ➢ 2 tbsps. black olives, pitted and sliced
- ➢ 680g potatoes, peeled and cubed
- ➢ Salt and black pepper to taste
- ➢ 1 tbsp hot paprika
- ➢ 230 ml Greek yogurt
- ➢ 1 tbsp olive oil

Directions:

1. In a bowl, mix the potatoes with the oil, salt, pepper, and paprika, toss well.
2. Put the potatoes in your air fryer's basket and cook at 200°C (390°F) for 15 minutes.
3. Place the potatoes in a serving dish, and add the yogurt and the black olives.
4. Toss, serve, and enjoy.

Nutritional Value (Amount per Serving):

Calories: 140; Fat: 3; Carbs: 10; Protein: 4

Grilled Mushrooms

Prep Time: 10 Minutes Cook Time: 20 Minutes Serves: 2

Ingredients:

- 2 yellow bell peppers, seeded and sliced
- 6 large Portobello mushrooms, sliced
- 140g shredded mozzarella cheese
- 120g Italian vinaigrette
- ½ tsp black pepper
- 4 eggplants, sliced
- 4 onions, sliced

Directions:

1. Preheat the air fryer to 176 °C (348°F).
2. Place the grill pan accessory in the air fryer.
3. In a Ziploc bag, put all ingredients, except for the cheese. Shake to combine.
4. Dump on the grill pan and cook for 20 minutes.
5. While still hot, garnish with mozzarella cheese.

Nutritional Value (Amount per Serving):

Calories: 212; Fat: 14; Carbs: 23; Protein: 13

Air Fryer Vegetables

Prep Time: 10 Minutes Cook Time: 15 Minutes Serves: 4

Ingredients:

- ➤ 1 Large Bell pepper
- ➤ 1 Large Onion
- ➤ ½ tsp Black pepper
- ➤ 1 tbsp Olive oil
- ➤ 1 tsp Seasoning
- ➤ 380g Broccoli
- ➤ 250g Carrots
- ➤ Salt to taste

Directions:

1. Wash and cut the vegetables into bite size.
2. Add them to a bowl and season with salt, black pepper, or any seasoning of choice, and olive oil.
3. Mix so that the veggies are covered in the seasoning.
4. Add the seasoned veggies into the air fryer basket.
5. Air fry at a temperature of 175°C (347°F) for 15 minutes.
6. Toss the veggies in the basket halfway through cooking so that all sides are crisp.
7. When done, take out the basket and serve.

Nutritional Value (Amount per Serving):

Calories: 120; Fat: 4; Carb: 19; Protein: 4

Green Beans with Shallots

Prep Time: 10 Minutes Cook Time: 25 Minutes Serves: 6

Ingredients:

- 450g fresh green beans, trimmed
- 1 tbsp sesame seeds, toasted
- 2 tbsps. fresh basil, chopped
- 1 tbsp fresh mint, chopped
- 2 large shallots, sliced
- 1 tbsp vegetable oil
- 1 tsp soy sauce
- 2 tbsps. pine nuts

Directions:

1. Preheat the air fryer to 176°C (348°F).
2. Place the grill pan accessory in the air fryer.
3. In a mixing bowl, combine the green beans, shallots, vegetable oil, and soy sauce.
4. Dump in the air fryer and cook for 25 minutes.
5. Once cooked, garnish with basil, mints, sesame seeds, and pine nuts.

Nutritional Value (Amount per Serving):

Calories: 307; Fat: 19.7; Carbs: 11.2; Protein: 23.7

Sweet Potato Fries

Prep Time: 15 Minutes Cook Time: 35 Minutes Serves: 2

Ingredients:

The Fries:
- 2 medium sweet potatoes, peeled and cut into sticks
- 1 tbsp. extra-virgin olive oil
- Freshly ground black pepper
- ½ tsp. garlic powder
- ½ tsp. chili powder
- Salt

The Dipping Sauce:
- 2 tbsp. barbecue sauce
- 2 tbsp. mayonnaise
- 1 tsp. hot sauce

Directions:

1. In a large bowl, toss sweet potatoes with oil and spices.
3. Season with salt and pepper.
4. Working in batches, spread an even layer of sweet potato fries in fryer basket.
5. Cook at 190°C (374°F) for 8 minutes, flip fries, then cook 8 minutes more.
6. Meanwhile, make dipping sauce: In a medium bowl, whisk to combine mayonnaise, barbecue sauce, and hot sauce.
7. Serve fries with sauce on the side for dipping.

Nutritional Value (Amount per Serving):

Calories: 690; Fat: 40.61; Carb: 35.39; Protein: 43.57

Easy Broccoli Patties

Prep Time: 10 Minutes Cook Time: 10 Minutes Serves: 12

Ingredients:

- 470g cheddar cheese, grated
- ½ tsp apple cider vinegar
- 1 tsp garlic powder
- ½ tsp baking soda
- 940g broccoli florets
- 290g almond flour
- 60 ml olive oil
- 1 tsp paprika
- 2 eggs
- Salt and black pepper to the taste

Directions:

1. Put broccoli florets in your food processor, add salt and pepper, blend well, and transfer to a bowl.
2. Add almond flour, salt, pepper, paprika, garlic powder, baking soda, cheese, oil, eggs, and vinegar, stir well and shape 12 patties out of this mix.
3. Place them in your preheated air fryer's basket and cook at 176°C (348°F), for 10 minutes. Arrange patties on a platter and serve them as an appetizer.

Nutritional Value (Amount per Serving):

Calories: 203; Fat: 12; Carbs: 14; Protein: 2

Goat Cheese Brussels Sprouts

Prep Time: 5 Minutes Cook Time: 15 Minutes Serves: 8

Ingredients:

- ➢ 450g Brussels sprouts, trimmed
- ➢ Salt and black pepper to taste
- ➢ 85g goat cheese, crumbled
- ➢ 1 tbsp olive oil

Directions:

1. In a bowl, mix the sprouts with the oil, salt, and pepper, toss well.
2. Put the sprouts in your air fryer's basket and cook at 193°C (379°F) for 15 minutes.
3. Divide between plates, sprinkle the cheese on top, and serve.

Nutritional Value (Amount per Serving):

Calories: 150; Fat: 3; Carbs: 4; Protein: 6

Sliced Potatoes

Prep Time: 10 Minutes Cook Time: 15 Minutes Serves: 4

Ingredients:

- ¼ tsp Black pepper or to taste
- ½ tsp Rosemary or Thyme
- ½ tsp Garlic powder
- ½ tsp Onion granules
- 500g Potatoes
- 1 tsp Paprika
- ½ tsp Parsley
- Salt to taste
- 1 tbsp Olive oil

Directions:

1. Peel the potatoes, wash them and pat dry with paper towels.
2. Slice the potatoes into even slices.
3. Transfer the potatoes into a bowl then add in paprika, parsley, garlic powder, rosemary, onion granules, black pepper, salt and olive oil. Mix till all well combined.
4. Pour the potatoes into the air fryer basket and spread them out.
5. Air fry sliced potatoes at a temperature of 180°C (356°F) for 8 minutes.
6. Bring out the basket shake it, and air fry potatoes for another 8 minutes or until the potatoes are tender inside and crispy outside.
7. Bring out the potatoes, and serve.

Tips:

If you prefer not to peel the potatoes, wash the potatoes thoroughly to remove any dirt on the skin then pat dry with kitchen towel.

Nutritional Value (Amount per Serving):

Calories: 131; Fat: 4; Carb: 23; Protein: 3

Wrapped Asparagus

Prep Time: 5 Minutes Cook Time: 5 Minutes Serves: 4

Ingredients:

- ➢ A pinch of salt and black pepper
- ➢ 8 asparagus spears, trimmed
- ➢ 220g prosciutto slices

Directions:

1. Wrap the asparagus in prosciutto slices and then season with salt and pepper.
2. Put all in your air fryer's basket and cook at 200°C (390°F) for 5 minutes.
3. Divide between plates and serve.

Nutritional Value (Amount per Serving):

Calories: 100; Fat: 2; Carbs: 8; Protein: 4

Brussels Sprout Crisps

Prep Time: 5 Minutes Cook Time: 20 Minutes Serves: 2-3

Ingredients:

- 225g brussels sprouts, thinly sliced
- 2 tbsp freshly grated Parmesan
- 1 tbsp extra-virgin olive oil
- Freshly ground black pepper
- Caesar dressing, for dipping
- 1 tsp garlic powder
- Salt

Directions:

1. In a large bowl, toss brussels sprouts with oil, Parmesan, and garlic powder and season with salt and pepper.
2. Arrange in an even layer in air fryer.
3. Bake at 180°C (356°F) for 8 minutes, toss, and bake 8 minutes more, until crisp and golden.
4. Garnish with more Parmesan and serve with Caesar dressing for dipping.

Nutritional Value (Amount per Serving):

Calories: 378; Fat: 24.26; Carb: 8.81; Protein: 30.78

Coconut Artichokes

Prep Time: 5 Minutes Cook Time: 15 Minutes Serves: 2

Ingredients:

- ➢ 2 artichokes, were washed, trimmed, and halved
- ➢ 1 tbsp coconut oil, melted
- ➢ 2 garlic cloves, minced
- ➢ 60g coconut, shredded
- ➢ Juice of 1 lemon

Directions:

1. In a bowl, mix the artichokes with the garlic, oil, and lemon juice, toss well.
2. Put the artichokes into your air fryer and cook at 182°C (360°F) for 15 minutes.
3. Divide the artichokes between plates, sprinkle the coconut on top, and serve.

Nutritional Value (Amount per Serving):

Calories: 213; Fat: 8; Carbs: 13; Protein: 6

Chapter 6: Desserts

Heavenly Melting Moments

Prep Time: 5 Minutes Cook Time: 8 Minutes Serves: 9

Ingredients:

- ➢ 3 tbsp Desiccated Coconut
- ➢ 150g Self Raising Flour
- ➢ 50g White Chocolate
- ➢ 1 tsp Vanilla Essence
- ➢ 75g Caster Sugar
- ➢ 100g Butter
- ➢ 1 Small Egg

Directions:

1. Preheat the air fryer to 180°C (356°F).
2. Cream the butter and sugar in a large bowl until light and fluffy.
3. Beat in the eggs and then add the vanilla essence.
4. Using a rolling pin bash the white chocolate so that they make a mix of tiny and small pieces.
5. Add the white chocolate and flour and mix well.
6. Roll into small balls and cover in the coconut.
7. Place the balls into the air fryer on cooking tray and cook for eight minutes at 180°C (356°F).
8. Reduce the temperature to 160°C (320°F) for a further 4 minutes so that they can cook in the middle.

Nutritional Value (Amount per Serving):

Calories: 147; Fat: 6.78; Carb: 18.23; Protein: 2.87

Walnut and Vanilla Bars

Prep Time: 5 Minutes Cook Time: 16 Minutes Serves: 4

Ingredients:

- 60g walnuts, chopped
- 60g almond flour
- 80g cocoa powder
- 7 tbsp ghee, melted
- ½ tsp baking soda
- 1 tsp vanilla extract
- 3 tbsp swerve
- 1 egg

Directions:

1. Take a bowl and mix all the ingredients and stir well.
2. Spread this on a baking sheet that fits your air fryer lined with parchment paper.
3. Put it in the fryer and cook at 165°C (329°F) and bake for 16 minutes.
4. Leave the bars to cool down, cut, and serve.

Nutritional Value (Amount per Serving):

Calories: 182; Fat: 12; Carbs: 3; Protein: 6

Cocoa and Nuts Bombs

Prep Time: 5 Minutes Cook Time: 8 Minutes Serves: 12

Ingredients:

- 470g macadamia nuts, chopped
- 4 tbsp coconut oil, melted
- 60g cocoa powder
- 1 tsp vanilla extract
- 80g swerve

Directions:

1. Take a bowl and mix all the ingredients and whisk well.
2. Shape medium balls out of this mix, and place them in your air fryer.
3. Cook at 148°C (298°F) for 8 minutes. Serve cold.

Nutritional Value (Amount per Serving):

Calories: 120; Fat: 12; Fiber: 1; Carbs: 2; Protein: 1

Sponge Ricotta Cake

Prep Time: 5 Minutes Cook Time: 30 Minutes Serves: 8

Ingredients:

- ➢ 7 tbsp ghee, melted
- ➢ 1 tsp baking powder
- ➢ 235g almond flour
- ➢ 235g ricotta, soft
- ➢ 3 eggs, whisked
- ➢ Cooking spray
- ➢ ⅓ swerve

Directions:

1. In a bowl, combine all the ingredients except the cooking spray and stir them very well.
2. Grease a cake pan that fits the air fryer with the cooking spray and pours the cake mix inside.
3. Put the pan in the fryer and cook at 176°C (348°F) for 30 minutes.
4. Cool the cake down, slice, and serve.

Nutritional Value (Amount per Serving):

Calories: 210; Fat: 12; Carbs: 6; Protein: 9

Avocado Granola

Prep Time: 4 Minutes Cook Time: 8 Minutes Serves: 6

Ingredients:

- 240g avocado, peeled, pitted, and cubed
- 60g walnuts, chopped
- 60g almonds, chopped
- 120g coconut flakes
- 2 tbsp ghee, melted
- 2 tbsp stevia

Directions:

1. In a pan that fits your air fryer, mix all the ingredients, and toss.
2. Put the pan in the fryer, and cook at 160°C (320°F) for 8 minutes.
3. Divide into bowls and serve right away.

Nutritional Value (Amount per Serving):

Calories: 170; Fat: 3; Carbs: 4; Protein: 3

Orange Poppyseed Loaf Cake

Prep Time: 10 Minutes Cook Time: 50 Minutes Serves: 6

Ingredients:

The Cake:
- 25g Poppyseeds, lightly toasted
- 130g Self Raising Flour
- 1 Orange, Zest only
- 130g Caster Sugar
- 130g Butter
- 2 Eggs

The Icing:
- 150g Icing Sugar, sieved
- ½ Juice of Orange

Directions:

1. Add the Butter and Sugar to a bowl and beat till creamy. Around 5 minutes.
2. Add the Eggs one at a time, beating after each addition until fully incorporated
3. Sieve in the Self Raising Flour and fold in along with the Poppyseeds and Orange Zest.
4. Line a loaf tin with greaseproof paper or a loaf liner or use a rectangular metal takeaway container. Add the Cake batter and level out.
5. Preheat the Air Fryer. Set to 150°C (302°F) and bake for 40 minutes.
6. Once it is ready, place the loaf tin in the center and leave to bake.
7. Check that the cake is baked through by inserting a skewer into the middle and ensuring that is comes out clean.
8. Meanwhile mix the Orange Juice and Icing Sugar together in a bowl.
9. Leave the cake in the tin until it is cool before removing. Top with Icing.

Nutritional Value (Amount per Serving):

Calories: 366; Fat: 19.8; Carb: 40.54; Protein: 7.58

Coconut Bars

Prep Time: 5 Minutes Cook Time: 40 Minutes Serves: 12

Ingredients:

- 175g walnuts, chopped
- 350g coconut, flaked
- 120g coconut cream
- 300g almond flour
- 235g butter, melted
- ½ tsp vanilla extract
- 235g swerve
- 1 egg yolk

Directions:

1. Take a bowl and mix the flour with half of the swerve and half of the butter, stir well, and press this on the bottom of a baking pan that fits the air fryer.
2. Introduce this in the air fryer and cook at 176°C (348°F) for 15 minutes.
3. Meanwhile, heat a pan with the rest of the butter over medium heat, add the remaining swerve and the rest of the ingredients, whisk, cook for 1-2 minutes, take off the heat, and cool down.
4. Spread this well over the crust, put the pan in the air fryer again, and cook at 176°C (348°F) for 25 minutes.
5. Cool down, cut into bars and serve.

Nutritional Value (Amount per Serving):

Calories: 182; Fat: 12; Carbs: 4; Protein: 4

Simple Shortbread Chocolate Balls

Prep Time: 4 Minutes Cook Time: 13 Minutes Serves: 9

Ingredients:

- ➢ 1 tsp Vanilla Essence
- ➢ 9 Chocolate chunks
- ➢ 75g Caster Sugar
- ➢ 250g Plain Flour
- ➢ 2 tbsp Cocoa
- ➢ 175g Butter

Directions:

1. Preheat your air fryer to 180°C (356°F).
2. Mix your flour, sugar and cocoa in a bowl together.
3. Rub in your butter and knead well until you have a smooth dough.
4. Divide into balls and place a chunk of chocolate into the center of each and make sure none of the chocolate chunk is showing.
5. Place your chocolate shortbread balls onto the cooking tray in your air fryer.
6. Cook them at 180°C (356°F) for 8 minutes and then a further 5 minutes on 160°C (320°F) so that you can make sure they are cooked in the middle.

Nutritional Value (Amount per Serving):

Calories: 331; Fat: 11.55; Carb: 51.01; Protein: 5.02

Lemon Bars

Prep Time: 10 Minutes Cook Time: 35 Minutes Serves: 8

Ingredients:

- Zest of 1 lemon, grated
- 120g butter, melted
- 410g almond flour
- Juice of 3 lemons
- 3 eggs, whisked
- 240g erythritol

Directions:

1. Take a bowl and mix 236g flour with half of the erythritol and the butter, stir well, and press into a baking dish that fits the air fryer lined with parchment paper.
2. Put the dish in your air fryer and cook at 176°C (348°F) for 10 minutes.
3. Meanwhile, in a bowl, mix the rest of the flour with the remaining erythritol and the other ingredients and whisk well.
4. Spread this over the crust, and put the dish in the air fryer once more.
5. Cook at 176°C (348°F) for 25 minutes.
6. Cool down, cut into bars and serve.

Nutritional Value (Amount per Serving):

Calories: 210; Fat: 12; Carbs: 4; Protein: 8

Sweet Zucchini Bread

Prep Time: 10 Minutes Cook Time: 40 Minutes Serves: 12

Ingredients:

- ➢ 120ml coconut Oil, melted
- ➢ 235g zucchini, shredded
- ➢ 2 tsp baking powder
- ➢ 1 tsp vanilla extract
- ➢ 1 tbsp lemon zest
- ➢ 1 tsp lemon juice
- ➢ 2g almond flour
- ➢ 3 eggs, whisked
- ➢ 175g swerve
- ➢ Cooking spray

Directions:

1. Take a bowl and mix all the ingredients except the cooking spray and stir well.
2. Grease a loaf pan that fits the air fryer with the cooking spray, line it with parchment paper and pour the loaf mix inside.
3. Put the pan in the air fryer and cook at 165°C (329°F) for 40 minutes.
4. Cool down, slice, and serve.

Nutritional Value (Amount per Serving):

Calories: 143; Fat: 11; Carbs: 3; Protein: 3

Sticky Toffee Pudding with Hot Toffee Sauce

Prep Time: 20 Minutes Cook Time: 30 Minutes Serves: 6

Ingredients:

Traybake:

- 115g dried stoned dates, roughly chopped
- 115g butter, plus extra for greasing
- 50g pecan nuts, roughly chopped
- 55g golden caster sugar
- 55g soft brown sugar
- ½ tsp baking powder
- 50ml boiling water
- 2 medium eggs
- 115g SR flour

Toffee Sauce:

- 150g soft dark brown sugar
- 80g unsalted butter
- 150ml single cream

Directions:

1. Place the dates in a small bowl and pour over the boiling water.
2. Leave to stand for about 15 minutes, until the dates absorb the water. Mash with a fork, then leave to cool completely.
3. Grease and line a 20cm x 3cm square cake tin with parchment paper.
4. In a bowl, beat the butter, caster sugar and brown sugar with an electric whisk for 2-3 minutes, until light and fluffy.
5. Add the eggs, dates, flour and baking powder and beat the mixture for 1-2 minutes, until well blended. Gently stir in the pecan nuts.
6. Set the air fryer temperature to 170°C (338°F) and preheat for 3 minutes. Meanwhile, spoon the cake mixture into the prepared tin and level the top with the back of a spoon.
7. Bake in the preheated air fryer for 25-30 minutes, until well risen, golden brown and firm to the touch. Insert a skewer into

the center of the cake, it should come out clean if cooked.

8. To prepare the toffee sauce, place all of the ingredients into a saucepan, gently bring to the boil then simmer gently for 5 minutes, or until the sauce has thickened.
9. Cut the warm sponge into portions and serve with the hot toffee sauce.

Nutritional Value (Amount per Serving):

Calories: 839; Fat: 43.62; Carb: 78.04; Protein: 37.13

Cocoa Cake

Prep Time: 5 Minutes Cook Time: 20 Minutes Serves: 8

Ingredients:

- 3 tbsp coconut oil, melted
- ½ tsp baking powder
- 1 tbsp cocoa powder
- 60ml coconut milk
- 4 tbsp almond flour
- 3 tbsp swerve
- 2 eggs

Directions:

1. Take a bowl and mix all the ingredients and stir well.
2. Pour this into a cake pan that fits the air fryer, and put the pan in the machine.
3. Cook at 171°C (340°F) for 20 minutes.

Nutritional Value (Amount per Serving):

Calories: 191; Fat: 12; Carbs: 4; Protein: 6

Almond Butter Cookies

Prep Time: 5 Minutes Cook Time: 30 Minutes Serves: 12

Ingredients:

- 235g almond butter, soft
- 1 tsp vanilla extract
- 2 tbsp erythritol
- 1 egg

Directions:

1. Take a bowl and mix all the ingredients and whisk really well.
2. Spread this on a cookie sheet that fits the air fryer lined with parchment paper, introduce in the fryer and cook at 176°C (348°F) and bake for 12 minutes.
3. Cool down and serve.

Nutritional Value (Amount per Serving):

Calories: 130; Fat: 12; Carbs: 3; Protein: 5

Yogurt Cake

Prep Time: 5 Minutes Cook Time: 30 Minutes Serves: 12

Ingredients:

- ➢ 1 tsp baking powder
- ➢ 225g Greek yogurt
- ➢ 255g coconut flour
- ➢ 1 tsp vanilla extract
- ➢ 6 eggs, whisked
- ➢ 4 tbsp stevia

Directions:

1. Take a bowl and mix all the ingredients and whisk well.
2. Pour this into a cake pan that fits the air fryer lined with parchment paper.
3. Put the pan in the air fryer and cook at 165°C (329°F) for 30 minutes.

Nutritional Value (Amount per Serving):

Calories: 181; Fat: 13; Carbs: 4; Protein: 5

Strawberry Cake

Prep Time: 10 Minutes Cook Time: 35 Minutes Serves: 6

Ingredients:

- 450g strawberries, chopped
- 3 tbsp coconut oil, melted
- 235g cream cheese, soft
- 2 tsp baking powder
- 1 tsp vanilla extract
- 235g almond flour
- 1 tbsp lime juice
- 1 egg, whisked
- 60g swerve

Directions:

1. Take a bowl and mix all the ingredients, stir well, and pour this into a cake pan lined with parchment paper.
2. Put the pan in the air fryer, cook at 176°C (348°F) for 35 minutes, cool down, slice, and serve.

Nutritional Value (Amount per Serving):

Calories: 200; Fat: 6; Carbs: 4; Protein: 6

Avocado and Raspberries Cake

Prep Time: 10 Minutes Cook Time: 30 Minutes Serves: 4

Ingredients:

- ➢ 2 avocados, peeled, pitted, and mashed
- ➢ 4 tbsp butter, melted
- ➢ 3 tsp baking powder
- ➢ 235g almonds flour
- ➢ 115g raspberries
- ➢ 4 eggs, whisked
- ➢ 235g swerve

Directions:

1. Take a bowl and mix all the ingredients, toss, and pour this into a cake pan that fits the air fryer after you've lined it with parchment paper.
2. Put the pan in the fryer and cook at 171°C (340°F) for 30 minutes.
3. Leave the cake to cool down, slice, and serve.

Nutritional Value (Amount per Serving):

Calories: 193; Fat: 4; Carbs: 5; Protein: 5

Currant Cookies

Prep Time: 5 Minutes Cook Time: 30 Minutes Serves: 6

Ingredients:

- 120g ghee, melted
- 1 tsp vanilla extract
- 2 tsp baking soda
- 450g almond flour
- 120g currants
- 120g swerve

Directions:

1. Take a bowl and mix all the ingredients and whisk well.
2. Spread this on a baking sheet lined with parchment paper, and put the pan in the air fryer.
3. Cook at 176°C (348°F) for 30 minutes.
4. Cool down, cut into rectangles and serve.

Nutritional Value (Amount per Serving):

Calories: 172; Fat: 5; Carbs: 3; Protein: 5

Ten Minutes Smartie Cookies

Prep Time: 5 Minutes Cook Time: 5 Minutes Serves: 9

Ingredients:

- 225g Self Raising Flour
- 50g White Chocolate
- 1 tsp Vanilla Essence
- ⅓ Tube of Smarties
- 100g Caster Sugar
- 100g Butter
- 5 tbsp Milk
- 3 tbsp Cocoa

Directions:

1. Preheat the air fryer to 180°C (356°F).
2. Mix the cocoa, flour and sugar in a large mixing bowl. Rub in the butter and add the vanilla essence and mix really well.
3. Using a rolling pin smash up your white chocolate so that they are a mix of medium and really small chocolate chips.
4. Add the chocolate and the milk to your cookie mix and mix well.
5. Knead your mixture well until it is nice and soft and add a little more milk if you need to.
6. Roll out your mixture and using a cookie cutter form into nice biscuit shapes.
7. Place the Smarties into the top of the cookies so that they are half in the cookie and half out in the open.
8. Place the cookies into the air fryer on the cooking tray and cook for ten minutes at 180°C (356°F).
9. Serve with warm milk.

Nutritional Value (Amount per Serving):

Calories: 185; Fat: 7.27; Carb: 25.55; Protein: 3.81

Avocado Brownies

Prep Time: 10 Minutes Cook Time: 30 Minutes Serves: 12

Ingredients:

- 120g dark chocolate, unsweetened and melted
- 235g avocado, peeled and mashed
- 3 tbsp coconut oil, melted
- 4 tbsp cocoa powder
- 1 tsp baking powder
- ½ tsp vanilla extract
- ¼ tsp baking soda
- 175g almond flour
- 2 eggs, whisked
- 1 tsp stevia

Directions:

1. Take a bowl and mix the flour with stevia, baking powder, and soda and stir.
2. Add the rest of the ingredients gradually, whisk, and pour into a cake pan that fits the air fryer after you lined it with parchment paper.
3. Put the pan in your air fryer and cook at 176°C (348°F) for 30 minutes. Cut into squares and serve cold.

Nutritional Value (Amount per Serving):

Calories: 155; Fat: 6; Carbs: 6; Protein: 4

Mixed Berries Cream

Prep Time: 5 Minutes Cook Time: 30 Minutes Serves: 6

Ingredients:

- ➢ 56g coconut cream
- ➢ 340g blackberries
- ➢ 340g blueberries
- ➢ 170g raspberries
- ➢ 175g swerve

Directions:

1. Take a bowl and mix all the ingredients and whisk well.
2. Divide this into 6 ramekins, and put them in your air fryer.
3. Cook at 160°C (320°F) for 30 minutes.
4. Cool down and serve it.

Nutritional Value (Amount per Serving):

Calories: 100; Fat: 1; Carbs: 2; Protein: 2

Half Cooked Lemon Biscuits

Prep Time: 5 Minutes Cook Time: 5 Minutes Serves: 9

Ingredients:

- 1 Small Lemon (rind and juice)
- 225g Self Raising Flour
- 1 tsp Vanilla Essence
- 100g Caster Sugar
- 100g Butter
- 1 Small Egg

Directions:

1. Preheat the air fryer to 180°C (356°F).
2. Mix flour and sugar in a bowl. Add the butter and rub it in until your mix resembles breadcrumbs.
3. Shake your bowl regularly so that the fat bits come to the top and so that you know what you have left to rub in.
4. Add the lemon rind and juice along with the egg.
5. Combine and knead until you have lovely soft dough.
6. Roll out and cut into medium sized biscuits.
7. Place the biscuits into the air fryer on the cooking tray and cook for five minutes at 180°C (356°F).
8. Place on a cooling tray and sprinkle with icing sugar.

Nutritional Value (Amount per Serving):

Calories: 164; Fat: 6.81; Carb: 21.64; Protein: 3.62

Lime Berry Pudding

Prep Time: 5 Minutes Cook Time: 30 Minutes Serves: 6

Ingredients:

- ➤ 470g coconut cream
- ➤ Zest of 1 lime, grated
- ➤ 80g blackberries
- ➤ 80g blueberries
- ➤ 3 tbsp swerve

Directions:

1. In a blender, combine all the ingredients and pulse well.
2. Divide this into 6 small ramekins, put them in your air fryer, and cook at 171°C (340°F) for 15 minutes.
3. Serve cold.

Nutritional Value (Amount per Serving):

Calories: 173; Fat: 3; Carbs: 4; Protein: 4

 **Chapter 7: Frittatas, Quiches and Casseroles**

Spring Onion and Cheese Quesadilla

Prep Time: 5 Minutes Cook Time: 12 Minutes Serves: 4

Ingredients:

➢ 4 spring onions, finely chopped
➢ 200g cheddar cheese, grated
➢ 4 x 20cm soft tortilla wraps
➢ Salt and black pepper
➢ 4 portions mixed salad
➢ 3 tbsps. mayonnaise
➢ 1 egg, beaten
➢ 1 tbsp olive oil

Directions:

1. Place the grated cheese, mayonnaise and spring onions in a bowl, season with salt and black pepper and mix well to combine.
2. Lay the wraps on a flat surface, brush the edges with egg, then divide the cheese mixture evenly between the wraps.
3. Fold the wraps over like a pasty and press the edges down firmly to seal.
4. Brush the wraps lightly with oil.
5. Set the air fryer temperature to 200°C (390°F) and place the quesadilla onto the basket, making sure that they are evenly spaced.
6. Toast for 10-12 minutes, until the quesadillas are crisp and golden.
7. Cut each quesadilla in half and serve warm with a portion of salad.

Nutritional Value (Amount per Serving):

Calories: 425; Fat: 21.86; Carb: 32.3; Protein: 24

Rhubarb Crumble

Prep Time: 5 Minutes Cook Time: 15 Minutes Serves: 4

Ingredients:

For the topping:
- 80g cold butter cut into cubes
- 120g all-purpose plain flour
- 60g of light brown sugar
- ⅛ tsp of salt

For the filling:
- Spray oil or butter to grease ramekins
- 20g all-purpose plain flour
- ½ tsp of vanilla extract
- 150g white sugar
- 500g of rhubarb

Directions:

1. Pre-heat your air fryer to 190°C (374°F).
2. Get yourself a large mixing bowl. Combine together the white sugar, plain flour and vanilla extract.
3. Wash the rhubarb and remove the ends. Cut into ½-inch-thick pieces.
4. Add the rhubarb to your filling mixture. Stir well.
5. Place into the lightly greased ramekins.
6. Combine together the flour and butter, tile you have a crumble consistency. Add the salt and brown sugar and mix well.
7. Place this over the top of your filling.
8. Bake at 190°C (374°F) for 15 minutes.
9. Serve with lashings of custard and enjoy!

Nutritional Value (Amount per Serving):

Calories: 775; Fat: 22.74; Carb: 118.16; Protein: 29.14

Air Fryer Chimichanga

Prep Time: 15 Minutes Cook Time: 35 Minutes Serves: 8

Ingredients:

- 120g sour cream, plus more for serving
- 100g grated pepper jack cheese
- 560g shredded cooked chicken
- 1 small yellow onion, chopped
- Freshly ground black pepper
- 1 x 400g can refried beans
- 1 tbsp. extra-virgin olive oil
- 2 cloves garlic, crushed
- Guacamole, for serving
- 8 large flour tortillas
- 100g grated cheddar
- 1 tsp. chili powder
- 1 tsp. ground cumin
- ½ tsp. garlic powder
- Cooking spray
- 195g salsa
- Salt

Directions:

1. In a medium pan over medium heat, heat oil. Add onions and cook until soft, 5 minutes.
2. Add garlic, chili powder, cumin, and garlic powder. Cook until fragrant, 1 minute.
3. Add salsa and bring to a simmer, then add shredded chicken and toss to coat. Season with salt and pepper. Remove from heat.
4. Spread about 65g of refried beans in center of tortilla, then sprinkle with both cheeses.
5. Top with about 70g of chicken mixture and some sour cream.
6. Roll into a burrito by folding the top and bottom of tortilla into the center, then fold the right side all the way over the filling,

tucking and rolling tightly. Set aside on a plate, seam side down, and repeat with remaining tortillas and filling.

7. Working in batches as necessary, place burritos into basket of air fryer, seam side down, and spray with a little cooking spray.
8. Cook at 200°C (390°F) for 5 minutes, then flip, spray with more cooking spray, and cook another 5 minutes.
9. Drizzle with more sour cream and serve with guacamole.

Nutritional Value (Amount per Serving):

Calories: 783; Fat: 52.21; Carb: 28.95; Protein: 47.66

Egg And Bacon Pie

Prep Time: 10 Minutes Cook Time: 20 Minutes Serves: 8

Ingredients:

- Air Fryer Frozen Bacon
- 4 tbsp Skimmed Milk
- Air Fryer Pie Crust
- 1 Small Egg beaten
- Flour for dusting
- 9 Large Eggs
- 2 tsp Parsley
- Salt and Pepper

Directions:

1. Place your just cooked bacon on kitchen towels and allow the extra fat to soak into the towels. After 20 minutes remove the bacon and slice into chunks.
2. Flour a clean worktop and a rolling pin and then roll out your short crust pastry.
3. Line a quiche dish with short crust pastry and then add your bacon bits, spreading them out so that you will get an equal bacon spread.
4. In a jug add the eggs and seasonings and then beat and then add in the milk and carry on stirring.
5. Pour the egg and milk mixture over the bacon until you have an almost full quiche dish.
6. Then roll out the rest of the pastry and line the top of your egg and bacon pie.
7. Then brush on some egg wash and cut a few holes in the center to allow the pie to breathe as it cooks. Load into the air fryer.
8. Air fry your egg and bacon pie for 20 minutes at 170°C (338°F) and then keep it in the air fryer to set for a further 20 minutes.
9. Then you can remove the pie from the air fryer, slice and serve.

Nutritional Value (Amount per Serving):

Calories: 180; Fat: 11.97; Carb: 12.53; Protein: 5.48

Tortilla Pizza

Prep Time: 1 Minute Cook Time: 5 Minutes Serves: 1

Ingredients:

- ➢ 30g grated mozzarella cheese
- ➢ Pepperoni or other toppings
- ➢ 30 ml Pizza sauce
- ➢ 1 tortilla
- ➢ Herbs

Directions:

1. Place your tortilla on a chopping board. Spread pizza sauce over the tortilla.
2. Add the meat or other pizza toppings. Add the cheese last.
3. Either line the air fryer with baking paper, to prevent sticking, or use a spray oil to spray the entire air fryer basket. (I prefer to use baking paper, as it catches the mess and is very simple to remove from the basket with a spatula. I also use spray olive oil, though you're technically not meant to use this in the air fryer!)
4. Cook at 200°C (390°F) for 5 minutes.
5. Top with a sprinkling of fresh herbs (or dried work well too).
6. Slice, serve and enjoy! (It goes GREAT with air fryer garlic bread too.)

Tips:

If you don't have Pizza sauce in you can use a little passata and tomato puree mixed together OR even just use tomato puree and jazz it up with a little garlic powder, basil and oregano.

Nutritional Value (Amount per Serving):

Calories: 956; Fat: 32.49; Carb: 119.76; Protein: 45.28

Air Fryer Omelets

Prep Time: 5 Minutes Cook Time: 15 Minutes Serves: 2

Ingredients:

- 60g Chopped Cooked Meat (chicken, beef, sausage Optional)
- 2 sprig Spring onions chopped
- 2 tbsps. Whole Milk
- 1 Tomato chopped
- ½ tsp Seasoning
- ¼ tsp Black pepper
- Salt to taste
- Cheese Optional
- 4 Eggs

Directions:

1. In a bowl, break the eggs then add milk. Whisk till well mixed.
2. Add in black pepper, salt, chopped spring onions, tomatoes, and seasoning, Mix together.
3. Grease or spray the pan with cooking oil or butter. This is so the Omelets comes out clean from the pan.
4. Now, pour the egg mixture into the baking pan.
5. Place the pan in the air fryer basket and air fry at a temperature of 140°C (284°F) for 10 minutes or till cooked through and a toothpick inserted comes out clean.
6. Take the pan out, turn onto a plate.
7. cut up, serve and enjoy your Omelets frittata.

Nutritional Value (Amount per Serving):

Calories: 154; Fat: 9; Carb: 6; Protein: 12

Courgetti Fritters

Prep Time: 10 Minutes Cook Time: 15 Minutes Serves: 9

Ingredients:

- 75g Onion, peeled and diced
- 25g Cheddar Cheese, grated
- 1 Medium Egg, beaten
- 150g Grated Courgetti
- 1 tbsp Mixed Herbs
- 100g Plain Flour
- 5 tbsp Milk
- Salt and Pepper

Directions:

1. Put the plain flour into a bowl and add the seasoning.
2. Whisk the egg and milk and then add to the flour to make a smooth creamy batter.
3. Grate the courgette making sure to remove any excess moisture.
4. Then add the onion. Stir in the cheese.
5. If the batter isn't very thick then add more flour and cheese to it until it is of a reasonable thick mixture.
6. Make them into small burger shapes and place in the Air Fryer.
7. Cook on a 200°C (390°F) heat for 20 minutes or until fully cooked.
8. Serve them with a good dollop of sour cream or mayonnaise.

Nutritional Value (Amount per Serving):

Calories: 131; Fat: 5.65; Carb: 12.66; Protein: 7.29

Simple Frozen Samosa

Prep Time: 5 Minutes Cook Time: 20 Minutes Serves: 2

Ingredients:

> ➢ 4 frozen samosas
> ➢ Olive oil spray

Directions:

1. Spray both sides of the samosas with olive oil.
2. Place them in the air fryer. Do not stack them, if you have a lot of samosas to cook, do them in batches instead of stacking.
3. Set the timer to 20 minutes and the temperature to 190°C (374°F) and let it cook for 10 minutes.
4. Remove the fryer basket and shake it around to ensure all the samosas cook evenly.
5. Resume cooking for the remaining 10 minutes, remove again and check to ensure its brown and crispy enough for your liking. If not, cook for an additional 2-3 minutes.

Nutritional Value (Amount per Serving):

Calories: 198; Fat: 16.24; Carb: 12.25; Protein: 1.7

Grilled Ham and Cheese

Prep Time: 2 Minutes Cook Time: 10 Minutes Serves: 1

Ingredients:

- 10g margarine or mayonnaise your choice
- 40g sliced or grated cheddar cheese
- 2 slices of cooked ham of choice
- 2 slices of crusty bread

Directions:

1. Pre-heat the air fryer basket to 180°C (356°F) for 1-2 minutes.
2. Take your bread, layer up the cheese and ham. Make a sandwich up.
3. Spread the outside of the bread with the butter or mayonnaise.
4. Cook for 10 minutes at 180°C (356°F) and turn 5 minutes in. You CAN skip the flipping if you're short on time or effort as this only makes a very marginal difference to the cooking and browning of this sandwich.
5. Serve with a nice salad to make it more balanced.

Nutritional Value (Amount per Serving):

Calories: 295; Fat: 14.47; Carb: 24.57; Protein: 16.7

Sage Onion Stuffing Balls

Prep Time: 3 Minutes Cook Time: 15 Minutes Serves: 9

Ingredients:

- ½ Small Onion, peeled and diced
- 100g Sausage Meat
- ½ tsp Garlic Puree
- 3 tbsp Breadcrumbs
- Salt and Pepper
- 1 tsp Sage

Directions:

1. Place your ingredients into a mixing bowl and mix well.
2. Form into medium sized balls and place them in the Air Fryer
3. Cook at 180°C (356°F) for 15 minutes.
4. Then serve.

Nutritional Value (Amount per Serving):

Calories: 73; Fat: 2.55; Carb: 9.46; Protein: 3.52

Frozen Hash Browns

Prep Time: 1 Minute Cook Time: 15 Minutes Serves: 8

Ingredients:

- 8 frozen hash browns

Directions:

1. Add individually frozen hash browns to the air fryer basket.
2. Air fry at 180°C (356°F) for 15 minutes, and flip over halfway through.

Tips:

The hash browns should be crispy golden brown on each side. If not, return to the air fryer for a further minute or two.

Nutritional Value (Amount per Serving):

Calories: 62; Fat: 3.29; Carb: 8.08; Protein: 0.75

Printed in Great Britain
by Amazon

37077362R00059